GATEWAY DEVOTIONS

KNOW LOVE LIKE THIS

21 DAYS OF DISCOVERING GOD'S HEART FOR YOU

Know Love Like This: *21 Days of Discovering God's Heart for You*

Written by Robert Morris, Kemtal Glasgow, Adana Wilson, Steve Dulin, Lorena Valle, James Morris, Monica Bates, Phillip Hunter, Irini Fambro, Jeremy Meister, Dana Stone, Julissa Rivera, Janna Briggs, Sion Alford, Bridgette Morris, Matthew Hernandez, Elizabeth Demarest, S. George Thomas, Chelsea Seaton, Zac Rowe, Hannah Etsebeth, and Niles Holsinger.

Editorial Director *S. George Thomas*

Executive Director of Gateway Media
Lawrence Swicegood

Senior Director of Gateway Publishing
Stacy Burnett

Senior Editor *Katie Smith*

Project Coordinator *Chasity Walker*

Creative Director *Peyton Sepeda*

Designer *Emanuel Pușcaș*

ISBN (ENG): 978-1-956943-60-3
ISBN eBook (ENG): 978-1-956943-61-0
ISBN (SPA): 978-1-956943-62-7
ISBN eBook (SPA): 978-1-956943-63-4

We hope you hear from the Holy Spirit and receive God's richest blessings from this devotional by Gateway Publishing. Our purpose is to carry out the mission and vision of Gateway Church through print and digital resources to equip leaders, disciple believers, and advance God's kingdom. For more information on other resources from Gateway Publishing®, go to GatewayPublishing.com.

GatewayPublishing.com | GatewayDevotions.com | GatewayPeople.com

Printed in the United States of America | Miklis Printing, Inc. Garland, Texas (miklis.com)

Contents

Introduction

By Robert Morris

"For God so loved the world that He gave . . ." (John 3:16). There's no doubt that this is the most widely quoted scripture, and as a whole, the Gospel of John is the most read book of the Bible. But have you ever wondered why or taken a moment to learn a little more about the apostle who wrote it?

The Apostle John had a remarkable life and ministry. He was an ordinary young man who was privileged to walk closely with Jesus during His ministry on earth. He saw Jesus heal the sick, perform miraculous wonders, and step into glory on a mountain. John was also the disciple Jesus committed the care of His mother to when He was dying on the cross. And I believe, because of his close relationship with Jesus, John gives us insight into Jesus that's nowhere else in the Bible. It's the reason I tell new believers to start their journey by reading the book of John. Yet even those who've walked with Jesus a long time have so much revelation to learn from studying John's words.

John's Gospel account of Jesus' life on earth is different from any other book in the Bible and distinct in comparison to the other three Gospels: Matthew, Mark, and Luke. All four Gospels are books of good news, but while Matthew, Mark, and Luke are synoptic—or similar—John's Gospel is unique.

Matthew and Luke begin their Gospels with the birth of Jesus, and Mark begins his gospel with the birth of Jesus' ministry. But John begins his Gospel with the birth of time! In fact, only one other book in the Bible begins the exact same way as the book of John with the words, "In the beginning . . ." and that's Genesis. By tying his account of Jesus' life to the beginning of all creation, John was letting us know that Jesus wasn't only a man; He was also *God* in the flesh who had come to live among us!

We also know John wrote his book many years after the other three Gospels were written, which only cover the last year of Jesus' ministry while He was here on earth. Yet John tells us about events during Jesus' first *two* years of ministry that none of the other writers mention. (In fact, the primary reason we know Jesus ministered for three years is because John recorded Jesus observing and celebrating three different Passovers.) This is why John's Gospel is paramount to our study of Jesus' life.

John himself lived to be the oldest disciple (over 100 years old!), and he was the *only* disciple who wasn't martyred. All the other disciples died a martyr's death. So why didn't John? Because every time they tried to kill him, he wouldn't die! The same leader who crucified Peter upside down put John into a cauldron of boiling oil, but he continued to preach about Jesus while sitting in the oil! The leader was so intimidated, he took John out of the oil and banished him to the deserted Isle of Patmos, which was a place of exile for convicts.

John remained on Patmos for a year, which is where he wrote the book of Revelation. When he was released from exile, he returned to Ephesus where he spent the rest of his remaining days. For the last 10 to 15 years of his life, people would ask him to share his wisdom because he was the only person still alive who had walked with Jesus. Each time John would respond with these words: "Love one another."

In the final years of his life, he would repeat these words over and over: "Love one another. Love one another. Love one another." Finally, some people came to him and asked, "Why is that the only thing you ever say?" And he replied, "Because it's the Lord's command that we love one another. That is what He commanded us to do!" (see John 13:34).

It's clear to see that John believed the most important message he could communicate was *love*. It is *the* defining theme of his life and this Gospel. In this book alone, John uses different variations of the word "love" 88 times! And throughout it, he refers to himself as "the one whom Jesus loved." Now, at first glance, it's a little suspect considering John wrote this about himself. (It's kind of like Moses writing in Numbers 12:3 that he was the most humble man on the face of the earth.) For a while I wondered, *Why would he say that? Lord, did he not think You loved the other disciples? Did he think he was the only one You loved?* But the reality is the Holy Spirit inspired both Moses and John to write those words about themselves. And I believe the reason John referred to himself this way wasn't because he was trying to be exclusive. It's because John had the understanding and revelation of how much Jesus *really* loved him. It's as though he wanted to go around and tell everyone, "Hey, Jesus loves me! Can you believe that?! He loves *me*!"

My prayer is that you catch this same "He loves *me*!" revelation for yourself as you spend the next 21 days reading through the Gospel of John. I encourage you to let John's words about Jesus, inspired by the Holy Spirit, soak into your heart each day as you read through each chapter of John and *then* the devotion that corresponds with that chapter.

God's love for you is unconditional, inescapable, and unstoppable, which is why I love how the title of this devotional plays on the double meaning of "*Know* Love Like This" and "*No* Love Like This." My hope for you is that you'll truly understand that there is *no* love like Jesus' love for you and *know* His love in your heart. And through that knowledge, I pray you will also fulfill His greatest commandment, the one John stakes his entire life on: love God and love one another (see 1 John 4:21; Matthew 22:37–40). I truly believe if we would fulfill this one command, it would change the world!

1

Light, Love, and the Living GPS

By Kemtal Glasgow

And the Word became flesh and dwelt among us, and we have seen his glory, glory as of the only Son from the Father, full of grace and truth.

JOHN 1:14 (ESV)

Anyone who has ever spent time in the car with me would say that I tend to drive rather fast. Of course, the word "fast" is a relative term. If I were a pilot trying to take off the runway, I'd actually be going quite slow. So I prefer to say that I tend to drive "confidently." But while I always know my destination, I don't always know the step-by-step directions on how to get there. Some friends tease me that I'm "directionally challenged," and the truth is, I am! Without a GPS, I blow past exits and miss turns. Even *with* a GPS, I've heard (more times than I care to admit) the familiar refrain: "Recalculating."

And this doesn't only happen when I'm driving. I seem to get turned around while walking, shopping, and exploring just about any territory that's not familiar. During a season in my life when I was doing extensive traveling (more than 200 nights a year), I'd often get up in the middle of the night only to walk full-on into a wall because the night before I'd been in a different hotel room where that wall *was* a hallway! But on those occasions the problem in those hotel rooms was not that I'm directionally challenged. What I really needed was light.

In our lives, we need clear, safe, and reliable direction. But that's not enough on its own. We *also* need light to see the way!

The very first verse that opens the Gospel of John says, "In the beginning was the Word, and the Word was with God, and the Word was God" (ESV). In this verse, "Word" is referring specifically to Jesus. John 1:14 goes on to say that "the Word became flesh and dwelt among us." And Revelation 19:13 says, "And His name is the Word of God."

"Word" is also used several times throughout Scripture to refer to the *written* message of God—the Bible (see John 17:17; 1 Timothy 4:5; Revelation 1:2; Colossians 1:25). And in John 5, Jesus shows us the link between the written Word of God and Himself, in that He is the Subject of the written Word: "You study the Scriptures diligently because you think that in them you have eternal life. These are the very Scriptures that testify about me" (John 5:39 NIV). Did you catch that? Jesus is the Word, and you cannot separate His Word from Him!

You see, the Bible is not simply a book. It's alive (see Hebrews 4:12). What's more, it's both our light and our GPS.

Psalm 119:105 (ESV) says, "Your Word is a lamp to my feet and a light to my path." God's Word is living and dynamic, and the more you get acquainted with it, the more you'll get acquainted with Jesus. As you spend more and more time in God's Word, His thoughts about your future, His character, and His love for you will begin to unfold with more and more clarity, like switching on a light in the dark.

The Bible is also your GPS in that it helps you make great decisions because Jesus, the Word, lights your steps *and* guides you in the way of life (see John 14:6). God's Word gives you a glimpse of His unending, unyielding, and relentless love for you. Lamentations 3:22–23 (NLT) says, "The faithful love of the LORD never ends! His mercies never cease. Great is his faithfulness; His mercies begin afresh each morning." Romans 8:38–39 reminds you that absolutely nothing can separate you from His love! And because of His love, we can be confident we are being led the right way to the right destination.

I'm very thankful for physical light so I don't find myself walking into walls, and I'm thankful for simple directions when I'm going into new and unfamiliar territory. Today, you may need some spiritual light or some living navigation. Or perhaps you just need to remember God's loving-kindness and grace toward you. We all need to be reminded of that from time to time!

You can rest assured that, because of His great love, His direction for your life will lead you to victory over every circumstance and will guide you to abundant life. He who gives you direction and provides light to lead the way is indeed full of love, grace, and truth!

PRAYER

God, help me today to develop a love for Your Word and an inclination for Your voice and Your direction. I ask You, Jesus, to illuminate my path and direct my steps today. Help me to trust in Your direction for my life and experience Your great love for me. Fill my mouth with Your words and my ears with Your voice. In Jesus' name, Amen.

FOR FURTHER STUDY

Psalm 119:130
Hebrews 4:12
Romans 8:38–39
Ephesians 3:18–19

FOR FURTHER REFLECTION

Where in your life have you gone your own way and not allowed God and His Word to guide and direct you? What do you need to do to get back on track?

Have you allowed your quiet times to become a "to do" list rather than a dynamic exchange with God?

What could you do or say today to treat yourself like a beloved child of God?

LOVE

HOLY SPIRIT, WHAT ARE YOU SAYING TO ME?

2

Who Cares?

By Adana Wilson

Jesus told the servants, "Fill the jars with water." When the jars had been filled, he said, "Now dip some out, and take it to the master of ceremonies." So the servants followed his instructions.

JOHN 2:7–8 (NLT)

It was a typical Monday afternoon at the office. Typical in that it was filled with meetings. Then, out of the blue, I felt an intense pain in my wrist. As I listened to the gentlemen across from me, I slowly began to rotate my wrist, but I could barely turn it without excruciating pain. The afternoon melted into evening, and the pain only intensified to the point where I couldn't turn my wrist, and simply lifting my arm was horribly painful. I also noticed it had become very swollen.

Now, this wouldn't have been so mind-boggling if I had fallen or maybe won some kind of challenge in which I utilized my wrist (notice I said "won" because I do *not* like to lose), but I had done nothing that day other than sit in my office and have meetings.

Upon seeking the advice of a medical professional (whom I happen to be married to), we decided to make a trip to urgent care that evening. After an examination, x-rays, a steroid shot, pain meds, and a brace, the verdict was to follow up with an orthopedic doctor. As I lay in bed that night, not getting much sleep, I dialogued with the Lord about the pain I was feeling. I didn't want to have to find an orthopedist, follow up with them, or figure out what was wrong. I said, "Lord, I know people who are dealing with life and death situations right now. I've been praying for them! So, in the grand scheme of things, a painful wrist isn't that big of a deal. But I don't want to deal with this. I also know that You heal and You're concerned with what concerns me. Will You heal me?"

The next day, my pain began to decrease. By day two, I had no pain whatsoever. Months later, no pain, no follow-up, no figuring it out—total healing in my wrist!

In John 2, Jesus and His mother were attending a wedding, but then a problem arose—the wine was running out. In Jewish tradition, weddings were eight-day events that included feasts every single day. (All the people who don't like attending weddings, you're getting off so easy in today's culture!) And wine was a very important part of the wedding tradition. This wine wasn't quite like modern-day wine (in terms of alcoholic content), and it was instrumental to the meals and celebrations. At this point in the story, it was most likely only day three of the eight, and Mary was probably feeling somewhat embarrassed for the family (some commentaries say Mary and Jesus may have been relatives of the wedding party) because it was way too early in the celebration for the wine to already be gone.

So Mary brings the problem to Jesus' attention. But Jesus replies that it isn't His problem because His time hasn't come yet. Then two verses later, He quickly remedies the situation by performing His first miracle. He turns the water in nearby ceremonial washing jugs into not just wine but the very best wine at the wedding feast. Ultimately, what Mary was concerned about, Jesus was concerned about.

Jesus cares deeply about the things we are concerned about. Even the things that may not be life-threatening or life-changing. Running out of wine at a wedding feast was a big deal to Mary and those families back then, but it wasn't necessarily life-threatening to them, and it wouldn't have been life-changing if they had run out. Likewise, my painful wrist wasn't life-threatening to me that day, and if Jesus hadn't healed it, it wouldn't have been life-changing. But that day He reminded me by healing me that He truly cares about the things that concern me.

One of my favorite scriptures is Psalm 138:8, which says, "The LORD will perfect that which concerns me; Your mercy, O LORD, endures forever." The word "perfect" in Hebrew means "to bring to completion, bring to a finish or plead my case." Whatever is concerning you today, the Lord wants to complete it, finish it, or plead your case for it. It doesn't matter how big or small it is. If it is concerning to you, it is concerning to Jesus. He cares about what concerns you, so bring your concerns to Him.

PRAYER

Lord, thank You that You care about what concerns me. Your Word says that You will perfect (bring to completion, finish, or plead my case) anything that is concerning to me. I ask that You do this for me. I give those things to You: [name whatever is concerning to you today]. I trust You to move on my behalf because You care for me. In Jesus' name, Amen.

FOR FURTHER STUDY

Psalm 138:8
1 Peter 5:7
Psalm 55:22

FOR FURTHER REFLECTION

Write down the times Jesus has been faithful to take care of a concern you have had. Reminding ourselves of times when He has been faithful gives us faith that He will be faithful again.

Have you ever felt uncared for by the Lord? If so, ask Him in what ways He did care for you in that situation. Also ask Him to show you times He has cared for you and you may not have even realized it. Allow Him to bring truth, revelation, and healing.

LOVE

HOLY SPIRIT, WHAT ARE YOU SAYING TO ME?

3

Choosing Love

By Steve Dulin

For God so loved the world that He gave His only begotten Son, that whoever believes in Him should not perish but have everlasting life.

JOHN 3:16

John 3:16 is probably the most well-known and quoted verse in the Bible. If someone knows only one Bible verse, it's most likely John 3:16. This passage is so universally beloved because in it, God shares that He loves us with an almost unfathomable love; a love so complete that He sent His only Son to die for us so we might live with Him in eternity. The love referenced in John 3:16 is known in the Bible as *agape* love.

Agape love is the unconditional, self-sacrificing love given to others without expecting anything in return. It is the kind of love Jesus exhibited when He chose to die for us. The key word in the last sentence is "chose." Jesus made a decision and died for us, despite His emotions. But agape love is not only for Jesus to express.

God commands us in Matthew 22:36–40 to love Him, ourselves, and our neighbor with the same kind of love! You see, agape love is a decision. Love is an act of will. Contrary to what movies, books, songs, or culture tells us, it is not merely an emotion or feeling. We have to *choose* to love. And since this is a command, I decided to try to follow it.

After studying love for two years, I decided I would wake up every day and say, "Today, I choose to love God. Today, I choose to love myself. Today, I choose to love others." Sometimes, I said this multiple times a day. Each time I spoke those words, I was making an intentional decision to love God, myself, and others. One day, after about six months, I woke up and realized that I loved God, I loved myself, and I loved others. And it has never changed! Why? Because love is a decision. God wants us to love Him, love ourselves, and love others. But we have to *decide* to love.

My wife, Melody, and I have been married for more than 40 years. She is the love of my life, and she always will be. But early in our marriage, our relationship became very strained. While we'd made a vow to *love* each other, I am not sure we *liked* each other, and things were tense at best. One day we decided to go on a weekend retreat and just focus on intentionally loving each other. And you know what? We've both been in love ever since. I have made a decision to love her the rest of my life. You see, you can "fall out of love" if it's just an emotion or feeling. But love endures when you choose to make a permanent decision. Melody and I realized we had a choice. We could be married happy or married sad. We *chose* happy.

If you want to love, you have to decide to love. Colossians 3:14 says, "But above all these things *put on love* [make a decision], which is the bond of perfection" (emphasis added).

Even *Jesus* had to decide to love us enough to die for us. The Bible makes it clear it was an incredibly hard decision, knowing the path that lay before Him. Luke 22:44 says He was "in agony . . . His sweat became like great drops of blood falling down to the ground." But there, in the Garden of Gethsemane, Jesus *chose* to go to the cross because of His unconditional, self-sacrificing love for us.

No matter how difficult it may seem, I encourage you today—*choose* to love God, yourself, and others with agape love, and see what God does!

PRAYER

Father, by Your grace today, I choose to love You, myself, and others with agape love. It is a decision that I will reinforce for the rest of my life because I know it is Your will. Please help me to demonstrate and live out the type of love Jesus had for us on the cross. In Jesus' name, Amen.

FOR FURTHER STUDY

Matthew 22:36–40
Ephesians 5:1–2

FOR FURTHER REFLECTION

Do you love people based on your emotions and feelings or on a decision you've made?

Have you made a decision to love God, yourself, and others? Why or why not?

How can you demonstrate agape love to others today?

LOVE

HOLY SPIRIT, WHAT ARE YOU SAYING TO ME?

4

Simply and Honestly Yourself

By Lorena Valle

"It's who you are and the way you live that count before God. Your worship must engage your spirit in the pursuit of truth. That's the kind of people the Father is out looking for: those who are simply and honestly themselves before him in their worship. God is sheer being itself—Spirit. Those who worship him must do it out of their very being, their spirits, their true selves, in adoration."

JOHN 4:23–24 (MSG)

I was around eight years old and in line with 200 others to receive my first communion. I was so excited to wear a white dress, walk to the front of the church, and receive the sacrament. It meant I could take communion every time we went to church now, and I felt like I had arrived. As a little Catholic girl, this was a rite of passage! There was just one problem. For some reason, I had missed the classes required to receive your first communion. As we drew nearer to the front of the line, I realized that each person had to answer a question before receiving communion, and I had no idea what the question or answer was! I tried to listen to my best friend who was in front of me in line, but unfortunately, all I heard was "psssstttss." When it was my turn, I moved forward and repeated the same sound, and everyone laughed at me.

Nine years later, I remember sitting in a living room and hearing the story of Jesus explained to me in a song. That's when it became real to me. I thought of all the churches I had walked in and out of my whole life that had crucifixes on display, and I wept because I finally realized the reason *why* Jesus was on the cross.

Fast forward one year later. I was almost 18 and attending a youth conference. This moment is still so vivid in my mind, like it was yesterday. I was surrounded by the sound of hundreds of young people singing (what I now know as worship). The room was filled, and the presence of God was tangible. I had been a believer for less than a year, and my life looked less than perfect—I was in an abusive household, looking for meaning in my life, and full of insecurities. I had hit an emotional rock bottom. No one around me could tell. Everything on the outside looked normal, but on the inside, I was empty. Hundreds of people surrounded me, but I felt all alone. In the middle of my loneliness, I met with God. I had nothing else to lose, no one to impress. I didn't have anyone to help me make sense of my life, so I just started honestly conversing with Jesus. It changed everything.

In the last couple of years, the Lord has often reminded me of this memory. Do you have a similar one? When you hit rock bottom and Jesus met you where you were? If you've had a moment like that, let the Lord bring it to mind now. Let Him remind you why He died for you, so you could be honest and open with Him, and He could be your Savior—every day and in every circumstance!

John 4 tells the story of a Samaritan woman who meets Jesus at a well and has an honest and open conversation with Him. He helps her realize that God desires this from us—to be simply and honestly ourselves when we encounter Him. This woman had a religious upbringing, but she lacked an honest *relationship*. And that one conversation transformed her life. I relate so much to this woman's story because, like her, I first encountered God through religious rituals. But thankfully God's hand was guiding me even before I really *knew* Him. I remember our pastor once explaining, "Religion is man's attempt to get to God; Christianity is God's attempt to get to man." God sent Jesus to earth so we could have a real and unfiltered relationship with Him!

Matthew 11:28 (MSG) says, "Are you tired? Worn out? Burned out on religion? Come to me. Get away with me and you'll recover your life. I'll show you how to take a real rest." Jesus calls us to Himself, and in His presence, we can truly be ourselves. I encourage you today to have a conversation with Him like the woman at the well did. No need to use big words or complicated lingo. Just simply and honestly be yourself.

PRAYER

Jesus, I want to know You better. Today, I set aside any preconceived ideas about prayer and bring my true self to You. I pray that today my prayers become a simple and honest conversation with You. In Jesus' name, Amen.

FOR FURTHER STUDY

John 7:37–38
2 Chronicles 7:14
Psalm 27:8

FOR FURTHER REFLECTION

Remember God's promise today that as you get away with Him, He will exchange your burdens for rest.

Talk to Jesus about anything you're struggling with today. Remember to be simply and honestly yourself. And if you have a hard time talking honestly about your struggles aloud, consider writing them down. Journaling is a great way to express your heart to God.

LOVE

HOLY SPIRIT, WHAT ARE YOU SAYING TO ME?

5

Do You Want to Be Made Well?

By James Morris

Now a certain man was there who had an infirmity thirty-eight years. When Jesus saw him lying there, and knew that he already had been in that condition a long time, He said to him, "Do you want to be made well?" The sick man answered Him, "Sir, I have no man to put me into the pool when the water is stirred up; but while I am coming, another steps down before me." Jesus said to him, "Rise, take up your bed and walk." And immediately the man was made well, took up his bed, and walked.

JOHN 5:5–9

When I started working at Gateway Church, I was a stewardship pastor helping people with their finances. Whenever I'd meet with someone, I'd often begin our time by asking: "Do you want to be debt free? Do you want to be a giver? Do you want to have margin within your finances?" Many people were excited to say yes! But there were others who would give me excuses as to why the practical and biblically-based action steps we were encouraging them to take would never work for *them*. With those people, we had to *first* work on their perspective of God's goodness. Once they grasped that, we could discuss what they needed to change and what it would look like if they allowed God to take the lead. As people realized we serve a good, loving God who cares, they began to see that submitting to God meant more opportunities to see miracles in their lives.

The types of questions I asked people when I was in that role were similar to the one Jesus asked a sick man at the pool of Bethesda in John 5: "Do you want to be made well?" Interestingly enough, the response Jesus got back was not an enthusiastic "Yes!" either. Instead, He also received an excuse for why the man couldn't be made well. (Side note: The word *Bethesda* means "House of Mercy." And I believe that is what churches are called to be today—houses of mercy where people can come to receive and give mercy. Where they can come to be made well.)

Now imagine this: Jesus comes and visits you at church this week and asks, "Do you want to be made well?" What if He says more specifically, "Do you want your finances to be made well? Do you want your marriage to be made well? Do you want your health to be made well?" What is your response? Initially, we may all think, *Of course, I want to be made well! The obvious answer is yes!*

However, in the process of being made well, there is always an element of change involved. Repentance is needed—which involves fundamentally changing how you think and in turn, how you live. You cannot keep doing the same things you've been doing. If you want something you've never had, you most likely have to do something you've never done! In order to be made well, you have to allow the Lord to change how you think and act. For instance, if God is healing your marriage, that might include a process of healing your heart and changing your thought processes. You may have to talk to your spouse and treat them differently. Healing in your finances might mean you have to start spending, budgeting, saving, and giving differently.

This man at the pool of Bethesda was waiting for a move of God and a miracle. He had been sitting by the pool for 38 years! The sick man may have grown comfortable with his life situation and routine, or at least gotten used to the predictability of his situation. If he's healed, he'll have to pick up his mat and go to unfamiliar places. He'll probably have to get a job! He'll have to think differently than he has for the last 38 years. So I don't think Jesus' question to the man—"Do you want to be made well?"—was insensitive or irrelevant. All throughout Scripture, we see example after example of Jesus' love, care, and compassion for those who are hurting. There is *no* love like His! But He wants us to trust Him and be willing to live differently. And when we surrender ourselves to Him, we allow Him to bring lasting healing to our lives.

Jesus healed the sick man that day. The man picked up his mat and walked away—something he hadn't been able to do in decades! And do you know what he did next? He went and told everyone about what Jesus did! God wants to do the same for you today. He wants to heal you, and then He wants you to share your story with others so they can also experience His love and power.

So, I have some questions for you today. What are you waiting on God for? Do you want to be made well? Are you willing to take the next steps God directs you to take? Be careful you don't become so used to your circumstances or believe the lie that there is no other way. Let's not give God excuses or reasons why it won't work. Choose instead to repent—to change your mind and how you live. Listen to the Holy Spirit. He may be asking you to make a change in some areas of your life to better align with Him. Do you want to be made well?

PRAYER

Lord, I need You. As we read about You healing the sick man at the pool of Bethesda, I am reminded that You are a merciful God. You bless us with mercy and healing even though we don't deserve it. God, I am asking to be made whole, and I am willing to change my mind and live differently. You are the mighty One who heals. Please heal me. In Jesus' name, Amen.

FOR FURTHER STUDY

Psalm 103:2–5
2 Chronicles 7:14
Philippians 4:6–7
1 Peter 5:6–7

FOR FURTHER REFLECTION

Ask the Holy Spirit if there is an area in your life you need Jesus to make whole or complete. In your heart, respond and ask God to make you well.

Are there any steps you need to take or changes you need to make to better align yourself with God? Write down any thoughts the Holy Spirit brings to mind.

LOVE

HOLY SPIRIT, WHAT ARE YOU SAYING TO ME?

6

Exactly What We Need

By Monica Bates

And Jesus took the loaves, and when He had given thanks He distributed them to the disciples, and the disciples to those sitting down; and likewise of the fish, as much as they wanted. So when they were filled, He said to His disciples, "Gather up the fragments that remain, so that nothing is lost."

JOHN 6:11–12

Our youngest daughter Gabi was born about a month early. (However, she still weighed close to eight pounds!) A few days after we took her home, she appeared jaundiced, and our pediatrician told us to just make sure she was exposed to sunlight every day. But a few days later, Gabi appeared sleepy and weak, so we took her to the doctor again. After some testing, they told us to take her to the hospital.

When we arrived at the hospital, we were told her bilirubin levels were high, and she had to be in photo therapy for a few days until her bilirubin levels went down. The doctors were not very positive about her outcome. If the levels did not lower to a certain number, there would be severe things ahead.

Have you ever been in a situation where you didn't know if what you needed was going to be provided for you? Have you ever wondered if God was going to come through and take care of something in your life? Sometimes, in challenging times, the posture of our hearts can lean toward focusing on the severity of a situation instead of trusting God's promises and provision. When things are difficult, it's all too easy to lose focus of what you're believing for.

In John 6, we find Jesus up on a mountain with His disciples. (I think that location is somewhat significant since Jesus' view is always higher than ours. He sees things from an altitude we cannot, and He's always inviting us to come up higher than we currently are.) Anyway, a great multitude of people had followed Jesus to this place, so Jesus asked Philip, one of his disciples, where to buy bread so the people could eat. John gives us the inside scoop that Jesus was asking this to test Philip. Jesus already knew what He was going to do.

When you look at the life and teachings of Jesus, it becomes obvious that Jesus is *deeply* concerned about providing what we need. Why? Because His Father, our heavenly Father, is also deeply concerned about providing what we need. So in the middle of this situation, Jesus was testing Philip to see if he would believe the unbelievable. Can bread be provided for 5,000 people?

During those days we were in the hospital with Gabi, we had to battle fear and take hold of faith. We only shared her situation with those who had strong faith, would speak life, and chose to believe that Gabi's bilirubin levels would soon lower to the "certain number" needed. We *postured* our hearts and minds to stay focused on the *promises* of God's Word and His *provision.*

We stood in faith and prayed that God would heal her. And then we trusted that the outcome would be the best for Gabi and for our family.

After four days in the NICU, the doctors drew Gabi's blood again, and we were told her levels had reached the number needed for her to come home! We were tested, we were tired, but we had pressed in with everything we had to see God's goodness in our lives and in our daughter's life.

Jesus had the power to feed 5,000. He also had the power to provide for Gabi. Jesus knew the exact number she needed. We just had to make the choice to stretch our faith to match the truth of God's Word for her health and wholeness. And from just a little, He provided much.

Aren't you grateful that our heavenly Father loves us as much as He does and is always faithful to provide for us exactly what we need?

PRAYER

Father, is there is an area in my life where I need to walk in the provision, the posture, and the promise that You have for me? I ask You to continue to show Your grace and mercy to me today. Thank You for guiding me and leading me into all truth. Thank You for providing and caring for me. Thank You for being Jehovah Jireh, my Provider. In Jesus' name, Amen.

FOR FURTHER STUDY

Psalm 27:13
Psalm 34:8
Psalm 23:6 (MSG)
Philippians 4:19

FOR FURTHER REFLECTION

Ask the Father if there is any area of your life where you may not believe that He will provide for you. Listen to what the Holy Spirit says in response.

Ask the Father how you can posture your heart to receive His truth for your life today. Thank Him in advance for the provision in your life.

LOVE

HOLY SPIRIT, WHAT ARE YOU SAYING TO ME?

7

The "Crazy" One

By Phillip Hunter

And Jesus' brothers said to him, "Leave here and go to Judea, where your followers can see your miracles! You can't become famous if you hide like this! If you can do such wonderful things, show yourself to the world!" For even his brothers didn't believe in him.

JOHN 7:3–4 (NLT)

Has God ever called you to do something that your family simply doesn't understand? Have you ever felt like you're "the crazy one" to those around you? Well, Jesus can relate!

About 10 years ago, my wife and I felt the Lord leading us to leave St. Louis. It had been my home for more than 25 years. At the time, we had four children, and we were in the middle of adopting a fifth child. We were leaving most of my family, as well as our place of ministry, to come live in Texas. I didn't even have a job lined up. I was just believing and obeying the Lord calling us to Gateway Church.

When family or friends would ask us where we were going, we learned to say, "We feel the Lord is leading us to go serve at a church in Texas." We knew anything we'd be doing for the near future would be volunteering and not paid. And when we told people we were leaving a place with a secure job and moving to a place with *no* job, it was usually met with disbelief. The people we loved didn't understand how we could leave them or do such a thing to our kids.

But in that season, the Lord taught us an important lesson. God gives faith to those He calls for the specific season they are in. The particular level of faith we had for our move wasn't the same level given to our loved ones because it simply wasn't what they needed at the time.

Jesus' brothers and sisters had to know He was amazing. He was the perfect big brother. He never picked on them. If they asked to play in His room, He would always say, "Come on in." He was the big brother who wasn't sarcastic or mean but was always speaking life over them. Show me an awesome big brother, and I will show you little siblings who think he's their hero. I think Jesus' siblings loved their big brother but didn't have the faith yet to believe all the same things that God the Father had revealed to Jesus. In fact, Jesus' siblings even gave Him bad advice about His calling by recommending He go to Judea where people wanted to kill him! I don't believe they wanted Him to die; I just think they were unaware of the true journey God had for their big brother Jesus.

One of the hardest parts of our faith journey is learning to love and honor our family while also doing something that might disagree with their "uninvited counsel" or personal opinions. Has God spoken to you about a life decision and a family member is questioning your choice? Are you staying faithful to a marriage that your family thinks you should quit? Is God asking you to go somewhere that no one in your family has gone? Is there an area God has called you to that seems to disagree with family members' opinions?

Yes, it's important to seek godly counsel, and it's vital to always be submitted to the authorities God has placed in your life, but I want to encourage you not to get frustrated with your family if they don't have the same faith for something you feel called to. Loving your family and honoring them is always important, and God calls us to do exactly that. But don't let family be your excuse for not obeying God's voice. If God is giving you faith for something, and His peace is there, I believe God is in front of it and behind it, so go for it!

(By the way, my entire family now lives in Texas!)

PRAYER

Lord, give me faith to do what You're telling me to do. Thank You for my family and for filling me with understanding and grace to love them more. In Jesus' name, Amen.

FOR FURTHER STUDY

Matthew 10:37
Genesis 22

FOR FURTHER REFLECTION

Ask the Lord to give you wisdom and knowledge of His will for your life. Write down what He says. God doesn't lead by fear; He always leads by peace.

Bring any counsel or opinions from your family to the Lord. Are these family members actively praying for you and seeking God's counsel for your life?

LOVE

HOLY SPIRIT, WHAT ARE YOU SAYING TO ME?

8

It Matters How We See Something

By Irini Fambro

When Jesus had raised Himself up and saw no one but the woman, He said to her, "Woman, where are those accusers of yours? Has no one condemned you?" She said, "No one, Lord." And Jesus said to her, "Neither do I condemn you; go and sin no more."

JOHN 8:10–11

I remember the day it happened. I can feel the uncomfortable metal school desk underneath me. The smell of middle school boys around me who had yet to grasp the importance of deodorant. The sound of the overhead transparency machine humming. The taste of pure dryness in my mouth as the teacher asked me a question. Oh, and of course, the sight of my teacher staring right at me and asking if I could read out loud the math problem displayed on the wall in front of me. I squinted. I tried to scoot further up in my seat to see if I could get closer. I mumbled and stuttered a bit, "Ummm . . . uhhhh." I didn't have an answer. It seems simple now. I should have been honest and said I couldn't read the problem. But as an Egyptian growing up in Alabama, I spent my whole life trying not to be any more different than I already was. Yet, all my efforts did not hide the truth: I couldn't see the problem.

It matters how we see something. How I saw the math problem that day would greatly determine how I solved that problem. And I couldn't see the problem no matter how hard I tried. Because on that day, I cared more about how people would see me if I had to wear glasses than if I couldn't answer a problem.

It matters how we see something.

In John 8 we encounter a woman who was in pain. A woman who was in need. A woman defined by her present moment. Maybe that's not how you remember her story. Most of the time she is called "the woman caught in adultery." And that is how the people around her saw her, by her worst moment. If I'm being honest, I can do the same thing—see people through the lens of their worst moments. I noticed my problem the other day when I was listening to a sermon on Hebrews 11. At the mention of Abraham, I thought of how he lied about Sarah, which could have caused her to be violated by two kings. Later came David, and I thought about how he violated Bathsheba and murdered her husband. On and on the chapter mentions men and women of faith, and while the writer of Hebrews chose to mention their best moments, I saw their worst.

It matters how we see something.

Why did I see each character in the Bible from such a critical lens? Why do I tend to look at others in the same fashion? Maybe it's because that is how I look at myself.

It matters how we see something.

In John 8, the religious leaders saw a woman in her worst moment and defined her by it. They did not care to find the man caught in adultery. Just her. They defined her worth and value by her sin. But Jesus saw things differently; love does that. Jesus saw a woman who was hurting. A woman who needed to be protected, defended, and safe.

They saw her sin. Jesus saw her pain.

They saw her consequences. Jesus saw her need.

They saw her present moment. Jesus saw her possible future.

The people around her demanded Jesus see her by her sin. But Jesus instead asked the people if they wanted to be seen by *their* sin. One by one they saw her, and they saw themselves. They saw her sin, and they saw their own. They saw from one perspective, but love offered a different point of view.

It matters how we see something.

So here I stand in my present moment with myself and with others. How will I choose to see them?

Will I choose to see their sin or their pain?

Will I choose to see their consequences or their need?

Will I choose to keep them tied to this present moment or look to their possible future?

It matters how we see something.

Love sees differently.

PRAYER

Father, I come to You today spiritually near-sighted. Sometimes I get stuck seeing others from only their present or worst moments. Sometimes I see myself that way. Father, can You give me a fresh perspective? Make Your love so real to me that it changes how I see myself and others. Saturate me in Your love so I feel safe to bring You all my pain, need, and hopes for the future. Help me to see through the eyes of Your love. In Jesus' name, Amen.

FOR FURTHER STUDY

1 John 3:1
1 Samuel 16:7
Jeremiah 29:11
Ephesians 2:10
2 Corinthians 5:17

FOR FURTHER REFLECTION

Is there an area of your life that you think about often? It can be in your personal life, professional life, spiritual life, etc. Ask yourself . . .

- *Am I too hard on myself in this area?*
- *Do I avoid talking about this area with others or talk too much about it?*
- *How would Jesus see this part of my life?*
- *What would Jesus say to me right now?*

LOVE

HOLY SPIRIT, WHAT ARE YOU SAYING TO ME?

9

The Wrong Question

By Jeremy Meister

Walking down the street, Jesus saw a man blind from birth. His disciples asked, "Rabbi, who sinned: this man or his parents, causing him to be born blind?" Jesus said, "You're asking the wrong question. You're looking for someone to blame. There is no such cause-effect here. Look instead for what God can do."

JOHN 9:1–3 (MSG)

The ninth chapter of John tells us the story of a blind man who encountered Jesus. Spoiler alert: Jesus heals the blind man. But what follows in the rest of the chapter are some of the most hilarious interactions and conversations in all of the Bible. I highly recommend reading the whole chapter if you need a good laugh. But today, I want to focus on the first three verses. They provide the setting for the story.

I *love* stories. Stories give us a frame of reference, a context for our own lives and the lives of those around us. Stories connect us to each other. We all have a story. Whenever I sit down with someone for coffee or meet someone new in the church lobby or while I'm out and about, often my first request is, "Tell me your story." I want to know who they are, what makes them tick, and what God is doing in their lives.

The blind man in John 9 also had a story, although the details are sparse. We know he was blind from birth. We know from verse 8 that he was a beggar and had neighbors. We know from verse 22 that he had parents who didn't support him because they feared being kicked out of the synagogue. But what else do we know about his story? I wonder what his life was like. What was his childhood like? Was he teased growing up? How was his relationship with his parents? Where did he live? Was he married? Did he have children? Did he have any friends?

When the disciples saw the beggar, they didn't approach him with curiosity or compassion. Instead, they approached him as a theological problem. You see, the religious leaders of Jesus' day taught that all suffering was punishment for sin of one kind or another. There is always someone to blame. Someone is at fault. And they asked Jesus to help solve their theological problem, "Rabbi, who sinned: this man or his parents, causing him to be born blind?"

While we may not be able to relate to the blind man's exact circumstances, we have all faced pain, loss, heartache, wounding, betrayal, sickness, or disappointment in our own stories. Maybe we've experienced physical, emotional, or mental disabilities. And often, we respond to our stories like the disciples did: *How did things get this way? How did this happen? Why am I dealing with this issue? What is going on? Is it because I'm so messed up? Is it because of my family background?* We either look for someone to blame or we blame ourselves.

But Jesus doesn't seem to be concerned with solving the disciples' theological dilemma.

Instead, He comes in with all His goodness and kindness and says, "You're asking the wrong question. You're looking for someone to blame. There is no cause-and-effect here. Look instead for what God can do." Another translation says, "But this happened so that the works of God might be displayed in him." Jesus changes their paradigm, their way of looking at things.

Today, Jesus is still saying to us, "This happened so that the works of God might be displayed in *you*." According to Luke 4:18, He wants to mend your broken heart, set you free from oppression, and heal you physically and emotionally. But He also wants to change your perspective. Don't look to solve the theological dilemma of your circumstances or search for someone to blame. Look instead for God's good works to be displayed in your story.

Jesus changed how the blind man saw things. And in changing the way the blind man sees, He also changes how we all see.

PRAYER

Lord, thank You for Your work in my life and family. I ask that my life would be a display of Your goodness and power. Reveal those places in me where You want to change my perspective. Continue to work in me and help me surrender every aspect of my life to You. In Jesus' name, Amen.

FOR FURTHER STUDY

Romans 12:1–2
Philippians 1:6
Philippians 2:12–13
2 Corinthians 3:17–18

FOR FURTHER REFLECTION

Jesus wants to change how you see your circumstances. Ask Him to give you His perspective and write down what He says.

Where do you need healing—physically, emotionally, or spiritually? Thank Jesus today that He is your healer.

LOVE

HOLY SPIRIT, WHAT ARE YOU SAYING TO ME?

10

Dad's Whistle

By Dana Stone

"My sheep listen to my voice; I know them, and they follow me. I give them eternal life, and they shall never perish; no one will snatch them out of my hand."

JOHN 10:27–28 (NIV)

My husband and I have four children, and we've always been a very close-knit, active family. In our kids' younger years, we were constantly on the move between sports, school events, and many family activities and trips. Trying to keep up with all of them was challenging! If we were watching one child in a game, the others would often wander off to play with other kids; if we were on vacation, they would sometimes get ahead of us or lag behind us, blissfully unaware of their surroundings. Like most kids, they sometimes resembled sheep, aimlessly wandering from place to place, with no real destination in mind.

We did our best to keep an eye on them, but we didn't always succeed. When those moments happened, there was always one thing that would get our children's attention within mere seconds: Daddy's whistle.

This wasn't a shiny silver metal whistle that coaches use. This whistle was made the old-fashioned way: two fingers in his mouth. My husband's whistle is so loud, sharp, and distinct, our kids recognize it instantly.

We could be around hundreds of people with noise everywhere, and all my husband had to do was whistle one time, and our kids would immediately turn to look for him. Because of the deep connection they had with him and the trust he'd established with them, they recognized the importance of giving their full attention to his whistle. They understood that his whistle signified three things: information, instruction, and safety. They knew that when Dad whistled, he needed to tell them something, he needed to correct something, or he was keeping them safe from something. As the shepherd to our little "flock," his whistle brought stability and security because they knew he would always lead them to safe pastures.

Did you know you can experience that same stability and security in your own life? You can be confident you will be led to safe pastures? In John 10, Jesus told the story of a good shepherd and the sheep that follow his voice. Jesus said, "The one who enters by the gate is the shepherd of the sheep. The gatekeeper opens the gate for him, and the sheep listen to his voice. He calls his own sheep by name and leads them out. When he has brought out all his own, he goes on ahead of them, and his sheep follow him because they know his voice" (John 10:2–4 NIV). Jesus is our Good Shepherd, and He longs for us—His sheep—to hear, recognize, and follow His voice.

My kids knew my husband's whistle because they spent time with him. When we commit to walking in a covenant relationship with Jesus, we will learn how to recognize His voice too. Our trust and faith in His voice grow and deepen by reading His Word, staying in conversation with Him through prayer, and leaning into the wisdom and guidance of the Holy Spirit.

As our relationship with the Lord matures, we also acquire the ability to discern between the Shepherd's voice and the voice of the thief, who "comes only to steal and kill and destroy" (John 10:10 NIV). Satan wants nothing more than to fill our life with so much confusion and chaos that it robs us of the ability to hear the Father's voice. But Jesus' voice speaks love, peace, and purpose. It silences the lies of the enemy and allows His truth to bring freedom, hope, and joy to our souls.

Like my husband's whistle called our kids to come to him, the Good Shepherd is constantly calling His sheep to follow Him and experience a life so full and so free that nothing can pull us away from His side. Can you hear Him? He's calling your name. Draw near to Him, follow His voice, and He will lead you to safe pastures.

PRAYER

Father, thank You for being my Good Shepherd. I desire to hear Your voice more clearly and walk more closely with You. Holy Spirit, open my ears to Your wisdom and guidance so I can overcome the lies of the enemy and stand firm in the truth that You will lead me to safe pastures, here on earth and for all eternity. In Jesus' name, Amen.

FOR FURTHER STUDY

Isaiah 40:11
Ezekiel 34:11–16
Psalm 23
Revelation 7:17

FOR FURTHER REFLECTION

Read John 10 and write down all the characteristics of the Good Shepherd, what He does for His sheep, and how His sheep respond to His voice.

Set a few minutes aside each day and ask God to speak to you. Practice hearing His voice and write down what He says to you.

What is the Holy Spirit saying to you about the importance of recognizing and following His voice?

LOVE

HOLY SPIRIT, WHAT ARE YOU SAYING TO ME?

11

Believe, *Then* See

By Julissa Rivera

Jesus said to her, "Did I not say to you that if you believe [in Me], you will see the glory of God [the expression of His excellence]?"

JOHN 11:40 (AMP)

We began the journey toward our dream of purchasing our first home in February 2000. As we sat with our loan officer, I couldn't help but kick my husband, Mike, under the table while trying to keep a straight face. I had just heard him confidently say, "We'll have 20 percent of the down payment for the home in two weeks." We shook her hand as I silently thought, *This man has lost his mind!*

After quickly waddling my very pregnant self out of the bank, I looked at Mike and with a very passionate tone asked, "What were you thinking?! Where are we going to get that amount of money in two weeks?!" He looked at me with hope in his eyes, smiled, and said, "I felt faith arise in me. Julissa, there's nothing impossible for God!" Mike then went on to quote John 11:40, "'Did I not say that if you believe, you will see the glory of God?'" As I opened my mouth to speak, the Holy Spirit stopped me and asked, *"Do you believe I can do this?"* I remember taking a deep breath, closing my eyes, and whispering, "Yes, Lord, I believe You can. You have never failed us."

The words my husband declared in faith that day are the very same words Jesus told Martha as He stood in front of the tomb of her brother and His dear friend Lazarus. Four days had passed, and all hope was lost. Martha and Mary both struggled with the time frame in which Jesus showed up. The people of the village were also perplexed with His delay. Everyone thought He was too late. He wasn't. God is never too late—He is always on time, even when His timing doesn't match our expectations.

Jesus purposefully delayed His trip to Bethany so we can believe for the impossible. According to Jewish belief, the soul of a person lingers three days after dying, providing hope for a resurrection. However, if nothing happened on the fourth day, that hope was as dead as the person lying there. Let's look at the scene:

> Jesus said, "Take away the stone." Martha, the sister of the dead man, said to Him, "Lord, by this time there will be an offensive odor, for he has been dead four days! [It is hopeless!]" Jesus said to her, "Did I not say to you that *if you believe* [in Me], *you will see* the glory of God [the expression of His excellence]?" John 11:39–40 (AMP, emphasis added)

What a declaration from Jesus! If you believe, you *will* see His glory!

When everything within our human strength or effort fails, it's an opportunity for Jesus to step in and do what only He can do. This is when He demonstrates His love, His power, and His glory.

The next time you see yourself standing before something you deem hopeless, lifeless, or impossible, I want to encourage you to believe and trust in God no matter what you see! Take Him at His Word! The story of Lazarus is a beautiful picture and reminder that God can bring life to any difficult circumstance or situation. We serve an all-powerful, faithful, and loving God who fulfills what He promises. He is able to do exceedingly, abundantly above anything we ask or imagine, if we just believe (see Ephesians 3:20). Trust Him! Faith is the key that unlocks His glory—an expression of His excellence and goodness in our lives. "And without faith it is impossible to please God" (Hebrews 11:6 NIV).

The story of Lazarus ends with God receiving all the honor and glory just as Jesus said it would. The miracle displayed through the resurrection of Lazarus caused others to believe in Jesus too.

Oh . . . and as for Mike and me, what seemed "impossible" on that day almost 24 years ago turned into the sweet miracle he had declared and we had believed for. It was the very thing God used to glorify Himself in that season of our lives, and our story inspired others to also believe and trust Him.

PRAYER

Father, I thank You because You are faithful, loving, and true. Today I ask that You help me believe and see past the earthly perspective in front of me. Let me see through the lens of faith. Lord, I trust You and Your plans for my life. I know there is nothing too difficult or impossible for You. In Jesus' name, Amen.

FOR FURTHER STUDY

Hebrews 11:1, 6
Matthew 17:20
Luke 1:37
Ephesians 3:20

FOR FURTHER REFLECTION

Read John 11:1–44 and underline or highlight the times the word "believe," or a form of it, is mentioned. Ask the Holy Spirit to highlight any areas in your life (personal, spiritual, or relational) that you need to trust God with or believe for. Make a declaration in writing and place it somewhere you can pray for it.

Think about a time you've seen God come through for you during seemingly impossible circumstances. Take a moment today to thank Him for His goodness and His faithfulness.

If you need a dose of faith, write out today's key verse (John 11:40) or one of the For Further Study verses. Then, say it out loud and keep it within sight so you can declare as often as needed. Let God's Word strengthen you!

LOVE

HOLY SPIRIT, WHAT ARE YOU SAYING TO ME?

12

The Comfort of Friends

By Janna Briggs

Then, six days before the Passover, Jesus came to Bethany, where Lazarus was who had been dead, whom He had raised from the dead. There they made Him a supper; and Martha served, but Lazarus was one of those who sat at the table with Him. Then Mary took a pound of very costly oil of spikenard, anointed the feet of Jesus, and wiped His feet with her hair. And the house was filled with the fragrance of the oil.

JOHN 12:1–3

In 2020, my husband and I went through the most devastating season of our lives. Within the span of three short months, our 19-year-old son and our 22-year-old son both ran ahead of us to heaven. It was so horrific we barely knew how to function.

But it was during that season that I began to recognize the value of my friends in a way I never fully had before. Friends who I could call and just cry with over the phone. Friends who showed up and let me be raw and authentic. These friends held my hands at the funerals of both my sons and have helped walk me through life since then. There are still times now that I call or text just to hear and feel the safety of their voices and the reassurance of their consistency. I never knew how much I would need the encouragement and comfort that comes when I am in the company of trusted friends.

In chapter 12 of the book of John, many people focus on the beautiful act of service and sacrifice that Mary did for Jesus with her precious jar of oil. I am struck, however, with something else. Jesus, knowing He was in the last days of His life on earth, intentionally *chose* to spend time with His close friends. Fully man, yet fully Divine, He must have been thinking about what was on the horizon for Him. The pain. The rejection. The grief. The end of His days walking on this planet were not going to be filled with joy but with anguish. And yet, instead of withdrawing and isolating Himself, He chose to be in the company of His good friends.

I wonder if they shared stories and laughter over the meal Mary and Martha made and served? Maybe they retold stories and recollected the moment Lazarus's life was restored. Were there moments of quiet where the group could tell something was on His mind? Is this what caused Mary to make the decision to break her alabaster jar and pour out the contents on Jesus' feet? She performed that selfless act in the middle of the meal. Did the atmosphere of the room change? Did everyone in attendance sense that something heavy was weighing on Jesus? Something tells me Jesus didn't pretend with them. In the chapter before this, Lazarus is explicitly defined as Jesus' friend. Of all the places He could go in His final days, He chose to be with His friends. I think they must have brought Him comfort.

My husband and I have found comfort in the presence of our friends so many times in the last few years. God's statement in Genesis 2—"It is not good that man should be alone"—doesn't only apply to a spouse. If Jesus needed dear friends, how much more do we?!

So where do *you* go when trouble comes? Of course, you can—and should—go to the Lord, but do you have friends you can reach out to when your mind and heart are troubled? Do you have someone you can call, text, or meet up with when everything in your world is turned upside-down and you just need someone to hold your hand? And on the flip side of that, are *you* a friend who is safe for others to come to? Proverbs 17:17 (NIV) tells us, "A friend loves at all times, and a brother is born for a time of adversity." God *designed* us to live in community and gather courage from the company of trusted friends, in good times and in bad.

Perhaps you're reading this today and longing for friendship, but you feel isolated in life. If you're struggling to find good friends, please do not give up. If you don't know where to start, a small group is a wonderful place to find friends! Seek somewhere you can be vulnerable and real. Somewhere you don't have to show off *or* downplay your strengths and giftings. Somewhere you can be who God made you to be. Pray and ask God to lead you to people you can learn, grow, cry, and laugh with.

We are *not* meant to do life alone. Just look at Jesus!

PRAYER

Jesus, You are my friend, and I thank You. Would You help me be a better friend to those around me and build more authentic relationships with others? When I have things I need to talk about, please help me to find trusted friends to confide in. In Jesus' name, Amen.

FOR FURTHER STUDY

John 15:15
Galatians 6:2
1 Thessalonians 5:11

FOR FURTHER REFLECTION

Take a few minutes today and write down times a friend has made a difference in your life. Thank the Lord for those friends and perhaps send them a quick note of gratitude.

Is there a friend you could reach out to and encourage today?

Ask the Holy Spirit to show you some ways you could find new relationships, perhaps in small groups, at church events, at work, or in your neighborhood.

LOVE

HOLY SPIRIT, WHAT ARE YOU SAYING TO ME?

13

To the Very End

By Sion Alford

He had loved his disciples during his ministry on earth, and now he loved them to the very end.

JOHN 13:1 (NLT)

I will never forget the first time I saw her. Eyes sparkling with ocean-blue flashes. Hair dancing across her forehead and down onto rose-colored cheeks where a contagious smile seemed to give me permission to open wide my heart and hold her for eternity. I had never felt that way before. I was awestruck. I was in love. I would love this beautiful lady to the very end.

At this point in our relationship, she had never done anything for me. She had never said my name. She had never given me encouragement or said, "Thank you" or "I love you." In all transparency, I don't think she even knew who I was or why I was so infatuated with her.

But I didn't care. I was dedicated to love her forever because she was my granddaughter!

What I felt for my precious granddaughter Adeline that day was not unwarranted. I loved her with an unconditional love that wasn't based on her actions, accomplishments, deeds, or even her love for me. It was based on an unshakeable resolve I possessed that she was undeniably special, chosen, precious, and destined for greatness. I didn't see her that day for who she was in the moment. I saw her for who she was to become!

Jesus felt the same way about His ragtag team of disciples. He had spent nearly three years teaching, training, laughing, and praying with these men. They witnessed Him healing the sick, feeding the five thousand, and even walking on water, yet they still fought among themselves for position and power (see Luke 22:24). Even at the Last Supper, one disciple openly rebuked Him, and another stomped out mad on his way to betray Him (see John 13). They didn't deserve Jesus' love. They had done nothing to warrant such love. But He loved them anyway. Right to the very end.

Maybe there is some kind of divine fusion between my love for Adeline and Jesus' love for me. I loved her before she could understand or express her love back to me. God does the same. Adeline doesn't necessarily deserve the love I have for her just like I don't deserve the love Jesus has for me. Nothing she does in her life can cause me to stop loving her. Likewise, God has loved me during my wanderings and my rebellion, my good days and my bad ones. God has never loved me because of what I could do for Him, what I could accomplish in His name, or how I could express my love for Him in worship. His love for me has and always will be undeserved and unconditional.

So is His love for you! He loves you for who you are today and who you will be tomorrow. He loves you because He sees your future, He has plans for your life, and He knows the potential that resides in you because He put it there! He loves you because you're His child, and He hasn't stopped loving you because of anything you've done. There is *nothing* that can separate you from Christ's love. He loves you to the very end!

PRAYER

Father, I acknowledge that You first loved me despite my actions, accomplishments, failures, and shortcomings. I know there is nothing that I can do to deserve the love You have for me. Today, I simply receive Your unconditional love. In Jesus' name, Amen.

FOR FURTHER STUDY

1 John 4:10, 19
Romans 5:8
Romans 8:35–39

FOR FURTHER REFLECTION

Have you ever held an infant child or grandchild and felt an overwhelming sensation of love for them? What motivated your compassion and love for them?

How are you and that infant alike in God's eyes? How can this realization help you to position yourself to receive God's unconditional love?

Ask the Holy Spirit to give you a new revelation of God's love for you today.

LOVE

HOLY SPIRIT, WHAT ARE YOU SAYING TO ME?

14

Break Me Off a *Peace* of That . . .

By Bridgette Morris

"But the Helper, the Holy Spirit, whom the Father will send in My name, He will teach you all things, and bring to your remembrance all things that I said to you. Peace I leave with you, My peace I give to you; not as the world gives do I give to you. Let not your heart be troubled, neither let it be afraid."

JOHN 14:26–27

As you read the title, I'm guessing you finished that famous chocolate bar jingle.

Not too long ago, I saw that my son had one of those candy bars, so I sang the jingle, stuck out my hand, and asked if I could have some of it. I could immediately see his hesitation and the internal questions arising: *Do I give up my chocolate? I love my mom, but giving her some means I won't have the whole thing to myself?* With reservation, he slowly broke off a small part of the chocolate and handed it over with a sheepish grin, knowing it was a half-hearted offering.

Sometimes I wonder if this is how we think Jesus responds to us when we ask Him for His peace. Do we see Him as stingy or even annoyed, like "You need my peace . . . *again*"? Let me assure you, Jesus does *not* feel that way toward you. He loves you and wants to give you everything you need for who He's called you to be and what He's called you to do.

The Bible tells the story about a time when Jesus went out on a boat with some of His disciples and they ended up in a storm. As the storm rages, Jesus is somehow fast asleep while His disciples are all but losing their minds over the situation. They are stunned and, frankly, appalled that Jesus seems so uncaring—He's sleeping through the chaos! When I read the words Jesus spoke in John 14:27, "Peace I leave with you, My peace I give to you; not as the world gives do I give to you," that scene of Jesus sleeping in the boat while a storm rages overhead is what I picture. I imagine being in a chaotic situation, and God's peace so enveloping me that I'm able to sleep soundly through the situation and not stress.

The dictionary defines *peace* as "freedom from disturbance" or "a state or period in which there is no war or a war has ended." But God's peace is not the same as the world's peace; it is so much more. God's peace is a blanket of trust and confidence in Him that completely wraps around us no matter what turmoil is happening in our lives. The peace Jesus gives us is *His* peace. It's not a break in the war; it's being *in* a war and knowing that God is so in control and loves you so much that no matter what happens, He will walk with you to the other side, and you will be okay in the end.

Storms and wars can play out in all kinds of ways in our lives. A storm can be a season of illness or recovery. A war can involve praying in faith that a child or spouse will come back to the Lord or make good decisions. Storms and wars are part of life. That's why 1 Peter 4:12 says not to be shocked or surprised as if something strange is happening when you face trials in this life. They're simply part of our lives as humans and especially as Christians. James 1:2 and 1:12 both talk about enduring troubled times, too. But it's in John 14 that Jesus gives us the key to peace in the midst of trials: the Holy Spirit. God has given us His Spirit to comfort and guide us as we go through the storms and wars of life.

Has someone ever given you something out of obligation? Maybe you got less than what was agreed upon or were told you would receive? Maybe it felt like a tiny smashed portion of a chocolate bar? Listen, God gives *not* as the world gives. What He gives is perfect. Not only that, He gives us His very *best*. He gave us His only Son as a Savior! He made a way for us to have relationship with Him, and He gave us the Helper and Comforter to be with us in hard times. Our part is to accept the gift of the Holy Spirit and wrap ourselves in His comfort and peace.

Are there any areas of your life where you're in a war or in the middle of a storm? Is your life in a tornadic uproar? Are things just a bit unruly? I want to encourage and challenge you to assess your life and see if there are any areas where you're not accessing the peace of God. Are there any places in your life where you're not allowing the Holy Spirit to have full access?

Open your heart fully to Him. He is in control, no matter what storm is raging around you. The world cannot offer you the kind of peace you need. God, however, is offering a blanket of His supernatural comfort and peace to you today. Will you accept it?

PRAYER

Heavenly Father, I give You full control of my life. I submit myself to You, and I submit my trials and stressful situations to You. I give you my worry, grief, anxiety, frustration, [add any other feelings you may have], and I receive Your Holy Spirit as my peace and comfort today. Thank You for loving me and giving me everything I need. In Jesus' name, Amen.

FOR FURTHER STUDY

Matthew 8:23–27
Philippians 4:6–7
James 1:2

FOR FURTHER REFLECTION

Write down two or three areas that are troubling you today. Ask the Holy Spirit to exchange your anxious heart for His peace.

Take a moment to invite the Holy Spirit into your day. Perhaps write out a verse about peace, journal your prayers to Him, sing a worship song, or simply sit in solitude with Him.

LOVE

HOLY SPIRIT, WHAT ARE YOU SAYING TO ME?

15

Growing Pains

By Matthew Hernandez

"I am the true vine, and my Father is the gardener. He cuts off every branch in me that bears no fruit, while every branch that does bear fruit he prunes so that it will be even more fruitful. You are already clean because of the word I have spoken to you. Remain in me, as I also remain in you. No branch can bear fruit by itself; it must remain in the vine. Neither can you bear fruit unless you remain in me."

JOHN 15:1–4 (NIV)

In the fall of 2021, my wife and I took a trip with our best friends to northern California to spend a couple of days in San Francisco and Napa Valley. I was born and raised in California, so any chance I get to go back is an automatic "yes" for me. Our drive consisted of lush hills, incredible vineyards, and those gentle giants, the California redwood trees. But this was more than just a fun trip for me. The destination, along with our friends who accompanied us, was very intentional. Earlier in the year, the Lord had been speaking with me specifically on the first part of John 15, and because of that, I had begun studying vineyards. I wanted to learn about the vines, the soil, the grapes, and everything in between. Going to Napa and seeing it all firsthand with my wife and best friends was the culmination of what I had been studying and learning. To say I was excited to be there would be an understatement.

When I think about that trip, I don't just think about the new experiences shared or the conversations had in our Airbnb. I don't just think about the best pasta I've ever had in a tiny restaurant called Cook in the town of St. Helena or the best fall weather that California has to offer. What stands out to me the most was the vineyard we toured on our last full day in Napa.

We walked row by row with our guide hearing about this specific vineyard and viewing the grapes still on the vine because they were in the middle of their harvest season for the year. It was there that the guide talked to us about the soil and climate for that year and what it meant for the grapes. He told us about the growing process and the pruning process. Pruning is not just something that's *encouraged*; it's absolutely *necessary* for the quality of the vine and the quality of the vintage. If a vine is not pruned, it can result in overcrowding and the suffocation of the grapes. Not pruning shows lack of care and knowledge of the vineyard. Then our guide said something that stopped me in my tracks. He said, "Sometimes we have to cut off what we think is good and prune for the growth we know is best." He went on to talk some more, but I don't remember much of it because right there, on that warm fall day, I was standing in a vineyard and having an encounter with God.

In John 15:2, Jesus says that His Father, the Gardener, prunes every branch that bears fruit so it will bear even more fruit. When I look back on my life, I realize that in seasons where I thought God was cutting me, He was actually pruning me. Times where I thought God might be hurting me were ultimately healing me. Now that I am on the other side of these times, I can see God's faithfulness and His love for me. But in the middle of those seasons, I had *lots* of questions.

Maybe you're there now—a place where the pruning may feel like a cutting. Let me be the friend to remind you that, as we remain in Him, our Father the Gardener prunes us because He loves us. A gardener who does not prune shows no care for his garden, and that's not who God is.

From my study of vineyards in 2021, I know that the grapes that produce the best vintages are often the ones where the vine has suffered. When the vine is suffering, it is forced to dig its roots even deeper in the soil for nutrients and growth. The end result is a great tasting grape and vintage.

If some of the best grapes come from vines that must dig their roots deep in the soil and go lower in the ground, and if pruning is necessary to the health of the vine, that tells me that growing looks a lot like shrinking. The same is true for us as followers of Jesus.

Whatever season you may find yourself in right now, right this very moment, dig deep, remain in Him, and trust that the fruit and vintage that's being produced in you will be more than worth it! Trust that our Father is the best gardener, and He only wants the best for us because He sees the best in us—for we are His divine image bearers. Have confidence that this pruning or cutting will shape you for what is best. In your shrinking, growth is taking place.

PRAYER

God, I thank You that You are the best gardener and that You prune because You love me. I choose to always place my trust in You and not in my circumstances. I submit my life to You in every season. In Jesus' name, Amen.

FOR FURTHER STUDY

Luke 13:6–9
Colossians 1:10

FOR FURTHER REFLECTION

Do you find yourself in a pruning season? What do you think God is trying to speak to you in this time?

Look back at your journey and the pruning or suffering seasons you have endured. What do you know about God now that you didn't know then?

LOVE

HOLY SPIRIT, WHAT ARE YOU SAYING TO ME?

16

I Am Right Here

By Elizabeth Demarest

"But very truly I tell you, it is for your good that I am going away. Unless I go away, the Advocate will not come to you; but if I go, I will send him to you."

JOHN 16:7 (NIV)

In 2018, my family of five moved from Louisiana to Texas. It was a *huge* adjustment. We loved living in Louisiana! We were near family, we had a large community of lifelong friends, and I had been serving in full-time ministry there for 18 years. It was home.

A few months in to our new life in Texas, after the initial excitement of our move had started to fade, I began to grieve the life I'd left behind. I felt a constant cloud over my head. I'd go about my day doing the usual mom things—getting the kids ready for school, dropping them off at carpool line—but countless mornings, I'd cry all the way back home. I went from being eager to step into my day and excited about what God had next to being an emotional mess in desperate need of counseling and healing. My overwhelming loneliness zapped my courage, my confidence, and even my dreams and hopes for the future.

At one point my sadness grew so potent that when I'd wake up and read my Bible, I'd long to see Jesus face-to-face. I knew in my heart that He was with me, but I physically wanted to be where He was—I wanted to go to heaven. This went on for weeks. I even shared it with my husband. (It must have made him nervous knowing his wife and the mother of his children wanted to go be with Jesus in heaven!)

One morning, I was sitting on my couch with a cup of coffee, reading my Bible, and praying as I had been for weeks—telling Jesus I was ready for Him to take me to heaven. Suddenly, I was interrupted by the presence of the Holy Spirit. It was a "take off your shoes for the ground you stand on is holy" kind of moment. Everything around me faded to a deafening silence. Even my thoughts escaped me (and that's saying a lot!). Usually, I hear the Lord speak to me through His Word, or I have thoughts in my mind that I know are from Him. But there have been a few special times in my life when I've actually heard the Spirit speak as if He was standing right beside me. This was one of those times. He spoke as a best friend and in a gentle whisper said, *"But I am right here, Elizabeth. I'm here."*

He wasn't mad or angry with me, but His voice sounded sad. I realized I had forgotten something He desperately wanted me to remember. Growing up as the daughter of missionary parents in the Amazon rainforest, I didn't have many neighbors or friends. But after I gave my heart to Jesus as a little girl, I'd go into the woods and build my own playhouse. There, the Holy Spirit became my imaginary friend—except He was real! We'd talk as if He were right there in front of me. He became my best friend in that rainforest, and He reminded me on the couch that day that He would always be my best friend.

As I recalled that cherished memory, His words, *"I am right here,"* wrapped His presence around me like a comforting blanket, healing my heart longing to go to Him. The distance I'd been feeling between us for so long was instantly closed. He wasn't only up there in heaven; He was *in me!* (see 1 Corinthians 6:19).

We have a God-given promise in John 16:7—a promise directly from Jesus that He was sending the Holy Spirit so we could have a personal relationship with Him. And when we open our hearts and receive that promise, the Holy Spirit can be our constant companion, counselor, and friend. What a comfort! God Himself is present and actually living in us, at all times—even when we don't feel His presence.

The words of Jesus, "it is for your good that I am going away," teach us *so* much about the importance of the Holy Spirit in our lives. You don't need to go to heaven to be with Him! Those words tell us we can have a deeper and more intimate closeness with God through the Holy Spirit living in us than we can with Jesus next to us. The Holy Spirit is our assurance of God's constant, ongoing presence in our lives.

I don't know what sadness, loneliness, fear, or grief you may be facing today, but run to the Holy Spirit as your friend and helper. Wherever you are and wherever you go, He is right there with you.

PRAYER

Holy Spirit, I need You today. Help me to realize You are here, living in me as a promise from God to be my comforter, my friend, and my advocate in time of need. I choose You as my lifeline. When I forget this truth, please speak to me and remind me You're right here. Make me hunger and thirst for Your presence above anyone and anything else in the world. In Jesus' name, Amen.

FOR FURTHER STUDY

John 14:26–27
John 16:13
Romans 8:26–27
Romans 15:13

FOR FURTHER REFLECTION

Do you believe it's better for Christians to have the Holy Spirit living in us than Jesus sitting next to us? If that's true, then how important is it for us to cherish our relationship with the Holy Spirit?

If you're not making time to be with someone you love, does that usually help or hurt your relationship? Do you think it's the same with your relationship with the Holy Spirit? Spend some time with the Holy Spirit today, and ask Him to help you become more aware of His presence on a daily basis.

LOVE

HOLY SPIRIT, WHAT ARE YOU SAYING TO ME?

17

That the World May Know

By S. George Thomas

"I am praying not only for these disciples but also for all who will ever believe in me through their message. I pray that they will all be one, just as you and I are one—as you are in me, Father, and I am in you. And may they be in us so that the world will believe you sent me. I have given them the glory you gave me, so they may be one as we are one. I am in them and you are in me. May they experience such perfect unity that the world will know that you sent me and that you love them as much as you love me."

JOHN 17:20–23 (NLT)

Once upon a time, there was a large family with many many sisters and brothers. These siblings loved each other *so* much. Sure, they didn't always see eye-to-eye on everything—they each had their own unique perspective. But one thing they *did* agree on was their shared love and respect for their father and their mutual love for each other. Everywhere they went, they couldn't help but tell whomever they met about how amazing and loving their father was and how incredible it was to be part of his family! They actively sought to find anyone who didn't belong to a family (because all of *them* had been orphans once themselves) and invite them to accept their father's offer to join their wonderful family. Far and wide, this family was famous for their love and unity with each other. It was their defining hallmark.

Now in a nearby city, there was *another* large family with many many sisters and brothers as well. These siblings (who had once been orphans too) also told others about their father who wanted every orphan willing to join his family. The *difference* between the two families is although these siblings *said* they loved each other, their actions didn't really line up with their words. Some siblings would passionately declare their love and concern for orphans, while at the same time be critical and combative toward those already in the family. Others didn't even bother to share the good news about their father with other orphans and instead chose to only associate with select siblings who shared their specific opinions and beliefs. They *said* they loved all their siblings, but then they'd snipe and bicker with them over who *really* knew how their father wanted them to live and behave. Far and wide, this family was infamous for their conflicts and infighting. It was their defining hallmark.

Now let me ask you this . . . which of these two families would *you* want to be part of?

The reality is every single one of us was once an orphan spiritually. But when you and I made the choice to receive the gift of salvation and surrender our lives completely to Jesus' lordship, He immediately grafted us into a glorious, beautiful, and ever-growing family—*God's* family. And because you're now part of this family, that means Jesus' heartfelt prayer for oneness in John 17 includes *you*—"I am praying not only for these disciples but also for *all who will ever believe in me* through their message" (John 17:20, NLT, emphasis added). That's *you*! That's *me*!

I have two incredible older sisters. Because we share the same mother and same father, that makes us siblings—we belong to the same family. As much as there may have been occasions when they didn't love that fact—especially when I was being a pesky little brother—there is *nothing* they could do to change that. They had no choice in the matter.

Nor do we.

God doesn't ask our opinion on whom He accepts into His family. We don't get a say in it—as much as we'd probably like to weigh in. So the question is, will you resist it or embrace it?

Long before Abraham Lincoln famously said, "A house divided against itself cannot stand," Jesus said, "Every kingdom divided against itself is brought to desolation, and every city or house divided against itself will not stand" (Matthew 12:25). I like how the New Living Translation puts it: "A town or family splintered by feuding will fall apart" (Matthew 12:25 NLT). When we squabble with or take potshots at our fellow brothers and sisters, it grieves God's heart. He doesn't want His children at odds with each other; He wants His children to get along and love each other. Because when we do, *nothing* can divide us! Pastor Robert Morris says this: "Do you realize our unity is the one thing Satan fears the *most*? He fears the Church saying, 'It's okay if you have some different beliefs than I do. We're still going to choose to walk in unity.'"

In the midst of personality, theological, cultural, or political differences, our love for each other and commitment to remain unified is absolutely *crucial*. It's why, in His final hours before going to the cross, Jesus was thinking about and praying for *us* to be unified! He knew how you demonstrate your love and unity with other believers is *more* compelling than even your love and concern for the lost. Our unity—our *oneness*—is our single greatest asset in convincing an unbelieving world to believe and trust in Jesus.

Now God is *not* looking for us to be uniform: where we look alike, act alike, walk alike, talk alike. Nor does He expect us to be unanimous and agree on everything. But His Father's heart *does* desire for *all* of His children to be united: *one* body, *one* heart, *one* spirit, *one* purpose. As one as Jesus is with His Father! That's some *serious* oneness!

Again, I just love how Pastor Robert Morris explains it: "The number one thing the New Testament Church had that we need today is unity. They loved one another. Prayed for one another. Shared with one another. Encouraged one another. Helped one another. Ministered to one another. *That's* what we need more than anything. The reason the power of God was *so* manifest in the early Church is because they were *one*!"

God is counting on *us* to show such unconditional love for one another within the body of Christ the world can't help but take notice—so "the world may know that You have sent Me, and have loved them as You have loved Me" (John 17:23). *That* is the irrefutable evidence proving beyond the shadow of a doubt that God so loves the world. And *that* is our winsome witness that will draw others into the family of God.

Will you be the answer to Jesus' prayer?

PRAYER

Father, I confess sometimes I allow my differences with my spiritual brother or sister to influence my unity with them. And there are times I've been critical and unloving. Please help me to remember that this person is also Your child and that my love for them is a winsome witness to the world. Show me how to love like You have loved me. May I be an example of what it looks like to walk in unity with all my spiritual brothers and sisters. I desire to be an answer to the prayer You prayed in John 17. In Jesus' name, Amen.

FOR FURTHER STUDY

1 John 4:7–21
1 Corinthians 3:1–11
1 Corinthians 12:12–31
1 Corinthians 13:1–13
Psalm 133:1–3

FOR FURTHER REFLECTION

Ask the Holy Spirit, "Is there any fellow believer whom I've been critical of or whom I've been unloving toward?" If He shows you someone, ask for forgiveness, and then ask Him to show you how to reconcile with that person and walk in unity and love with them.

LOVE

HOLY SPIRIT, WHAT ARE YOU SAYING TO ME?

18

What's Your Truth?

By Chelsea Seaton

Pilate said to Him, "What is truth?" And when he had said this, he went out again to the Jews, and said to them, "I find no fault in Him at all."

JOHN 18:38

I was sitting in the salon chair getting a crash course on what hair products to use on my frizzy red hair. Now, you should know that hair is not my thing. Actually, nothing in the beauty industry is my thing. Hair, makeup, trendy clothes, none of it. I would rather be in running shorts, a T-shirt, and flip flops. "You'll want to apply this to your ends," my hairdresser instructed. Trying to learn, I asked, "Okay, so I put it up here?" pointing to my scalp. She chuckled and asked, "Is that where you think your ends are?" I then learned that I was pointing to my roots, and the literal ends of my hair are my ends. Which does make perfect sense, but again, hair is not my thing. We had a good laugh that I thought the roots were my ends, and I jokingly said to her, "Well, that's my truth. My ends are actually up here."

We hear a lot about truth these days. Your truth, our truth, follow your truth, that's my truth—there's a lot of talk about truth! It's easy to think all this talk about truth and allowance for multiple things to be true is a new idea brought on by me and my fellow millennials, but "What is truth?" is not a new question.

In John 18, Jesus is betrayed and arrested, and now He stands trial before Pilate, the Roman governor. Only the Romans could condemn someone to death, so the Pharisees needed Pilate to find Jesus guilty. The conversation begins with Pilate asking Jesus if He is king of the Jews. If Jesus says yes, then it could be seen as a revolt against the Roman emperor, and Pilate could, according to their law, easily find Jesus guilty and move on with his day. But Jesus, not one to be trapped by a question, responds with another question. He essentially says, "Did someone tell you to ask Me that? Or are you, Pilate, seeking truth and want to know if I'm king of this world and who I say I am?" (see verse 34). Pilate responds defensively and asks Jesus what He did to be put on trial. As the dialogue continues, Jesus presents the gospel to Pilate and shares that His kingdom is not an earthly kingdom. He was born into this world to tell people the truth and everything He says is the truth. Pilate then responds with that familiar question, "What is truth?"

Truth is something we inherently seek. It makes us feel safe and secure. It gives us purpose and meaning. We want to know what is true of this world, what is true of God, and what is true of ourselves. With everyone seeking truth and all of us carrying our own perspective, it's no wonder we have so much "truth" floating around. If we're going to know the real truth, then there needs to be only one source, or what is called "absolute truth." That is not a well-received phrase nowadays. We live in a world (and incidentally, so did Pilate) that says, "Believe whatever you want. Whatever is true and real to you can be true." But that's not how Jesus saw and taught things. In John 14:6–7 (NLT), Jesus said, "I am the way, the truth, and the life. No one can come to the Father except through me. If you had really known me, you would know who my Father is. From now on, you do know him and have seen him!"

Jesus said there's one truth—*the Truth*—and it's Him! When we're seeking what is true about this world, we can read the words of Jesus and see the world as He did. When we're seeking what is true of God, we can look at Jesus, and He shows us the Father. When we're seeking what is true about ourselves, we see what Jesus says about us and believe what is true.

When you find yourself calling your roots your ends, or your ends your roots, and wondering what in the world is true, look to Jesus. He shows us what is absolutely true, and we can trust Him. Jesus is our source and guide to true abundant life.

PRAYER

Jesus, show me what is true today. Please expose any lies I'm believing and speak the truth to me. Help me to walk in Your ways and show Your love to everyone I encounter today. In Jesus' name, Amen.

FOR FURTHER STUDY

John 14:6–7
Psalm 86:11
1 Timothy 2:1–6

FOR FURTHER REFLECTION

Reflect on the truth you're seeking. Maybe you're wanting to know what is true about you or a situation. Today, ask Jesus what is true and allow Him to speak to you.

What is the Holy Spirit saying to you? Is there an area of your life where you're not walking in God's truth? Allow His truth to lead you to new life in that area.

LOVE

HOLY SPIRIT, WHAT ARE YOU SAYING TO ME?

19

Reverent Remembrance

By Zac Rowe

For these things took place that the Scripture might be fulfilled . . .

JOHN 19:36 (ESV)

In the early spring of 2004, movie theaters across the country were filling up with people from all walks of life. CEOs and celebrities filed in next to teachers and teenagers, each of them eager to take their seats and see the highly anticipated new film *The Passion of the Christ*. The crowds came not only for a theatrical experience but a spiritual one. I remember the holy hush that fell as the lights dimmed; the shock and tears at seeing such a graphic depiction of Jesus' sacrifice for us on the screen. As the events of John 19 lit up dark theaters across the world, our rightful response was reverent remembrance.

Before any biblical scholars or movie critics jump in with their points of contention, let's not get caught up in the details here. This entry in our devotional is *not* intended to spark any fiery debate about the film. Today, we're not going to rely on Mel Gibson's depiction of John 19. Let's instead ask the

Holy Spirit to take us on a sacred journey of remembrance.

John 19 opens on a gruesome scene. Can you see Him there? The Son of God is covered in blood and sweat, His frame exposed as He crouches on the ground. The flogging He has just endured is the maximum punishment allowed by the law: 39 lashes from a whip lined with bone and glass. His heavy breathing can be heard by those close by as the One who has never known sin raises His face again, revealing bruises from the blows He's received. One of the soldiers pushes through the crowd, revealing a crown of thick thorns he's twisted together. In a mockery of Jesus' deserved royalty, the brutal crown is pushed onto the head of the One who bleeds for their salvation. As they toss a purple robe on His back, they shout and slap His face with sneers of evil glee.

Pilate, a Roman authority, walks onto the scene to oversee the proceedings. In defiant opposition of his own ruling in this matter, the Jewish leaders gathered below his balcony seem fixated on one outcome this day: "Crucify! Crucify!" In truth, Pilate had been shocked when he asked Jesus to provide His own defense and was instead met with a silent stare so intense it seemed the Man saw his every thought. Pilate snaps his mind back into the moment at hand. Turning to face those gathered, he shouts, "Behold, your King!" This only incites the crowd to a greater volume and more violence. What else can Pilate do? He knows not that he is living out the fulfillment of prophecy and that each of these things has already been written. Ordering a bowl of water to be brought, he washes his hands of the innocent blood being shed and turns the King of kings over to be crucified.

Soldiers and citizens alike gather around the mangled body of Jesus as they force Him to carry the heavy cross. On the Via Dolorosa (which means "The Way of Grief"), the Man of Sorrows takes one excruciating step after another on the way to fulfill both His purpose and the will of His Father. Arriving at Golgotha, Jesus is stripped of His clothes and stretched out on the cross. Three nails are driven through His hands and feet, but it's the pure power of His love that holds Him there that day. As He hangs in agony, every vile and disgusting sin from all generations before, present, and yet to come is placed on His blameless shoulders. Becoming the atoning, cleansing, perfect offering, the Lamb of God's body was pierced, releasing blood that would purchase salvation for all who would believe.

Think about this: As Jesus took those stripes on His back, He was remembering that you and I would be healed. As Jesus hung on the rugged cross, He was remembering that you and I would be forgiven of sin. As Jesus lifted His head and proclaimed, "It is finished!" He was remembering that you and I would one day be with Him in paradise.

As we go about our lives today, let's return to a place of reverent remembrance of the price Jesus paid for us to be made right with God. Our beautiful Lord Jesus, Lamb of God, we do this in remembrance of You.

PRAYER

Jesus, thank You for Your sacrifice. I actively remember what You did on the cross for me. May I follow in the example of obedience to the Father that You displayed as You laid down Your life for the ones You love. In Jesus' name, Amen.

FOR FURTHER STUDY

Isaiah 53
Hebrews 12:1–4

FOR FURTHER REFLECTION

Read John 19 again and meditate on the price Jesus willingly paid for you to be made right with God. Then thank Him for His loving sacrifice, and seek today to be an example of His love to those around you.

LOVE

HOLY SPIRIT, WHAT ARE YOU SAYING TO ME?

20

Too Good to Be True

By Hannah Etsebeth

Now Thomas, one of the twelve, called the Twin, was not with them when Jesus came. So the other disciples told him, "We have seen the Lord." But he said to them, "Unless I see in his hands the mark of the nails, and place my finger into the mark of the nails, and place my hand into his side, I will never believe."

JOHN 20:24–25 (ESV)

Staring out the backseat window of my parents' sedan, I saw a bright light scanning back and forth across the darkened Kansas sky. Next to me sat my older brother, a very mature second grader who was 18 months my senior. Wondering what the light might be, I whispered, "What is that?"

He looked at me with a newfound intensity and gravely responded, "Oh! You haven't heard?"

"No . . . what?" I whispered.

"The gorilla escaped from the Topeka Zoo today. They've been looking for him all day, and no one knows where he is."

My eyes widened as I considered the repercussions of the news I had just received. And I knew one thing was certain: I would *not* be sleeping that night.

My brother, however, would be sleeping just fine. Because he knew what I didn't. He knew there was an airport nearby, and the searchlight was a normal part of the darkened skyline in that area. And he *also* knew that he had 100 percent made up that story about the gorilla. This pretty much summed up a large part of my childhood, growing up as the only sister with three brothers. Teasing was a form of love and a foundational part of my childhood, and I wouldn't change it for the world.

Whether a result of all the teasing I endured or some other reason, I've learned that a sense of distrust is my first response to news that seems to be too interesting, too exciting, or just too good. (Not excluding the first few moments of my husband's marriage proposal, to which I responded, "Really? Really? Really? . . .")

So, when I read John 20 and see Jesus presenting His resurrected body to His followers, I find myself sitting in a "too good to be true" moment. Thomas's doubtful response feels all too familiar with the "too good to be true" news that the Christ, the One he had seen breathe His last breath, was in fact alive. Could it even be true? Seemed too good to Thomas.

Thomas wasn't always a doubter. In John 11:16 we see a taste of his deep devotion to Jesus when he opposed the disciples who did not want to go back to Judea where they feared the Jews were waiting to stone their Messiah. When Jesus explained a bit more, it was Thomas who replied, "Let us all go, that we may die with Him." In this passage we see a submitted follower who was willing to obey Him even if it meant he were to die with Him. I can imagine the grief that must have followed Thomas as he watched the things that took place on Calvary and the grief he must have carried into the day his friends told him Christ was alive.

Perhaps you're familiar with a time like that: when someone tells you God can heal your broken heart or that your marriage can be healed or that God can answer your questions. It seems too good to be true, and in the aftermath of heartache, brokenness, and confusion, doubt comes.

After Thomas's declaration where he essentially said, "I'll believe it when I see it," *eight days passed*. Eight days of grief. Eight days of questioning. Eight days of watching his friends celebrate the miraculous that had somehow eluded him. Eight days of the in-between, standing between the heartache and the belief in the miracle.

And then he saw Jesus. His hands bore the marks, His side bore the scar, and Thomas believed.

Today, if you are sitting in an in-between moment, I encourage you to take your heartache, your questions, your doubt, and your pain to the One with nail-pierced hands and a scar on His side. He is comfortable with all of your questions. He understands where you are, and He's willing to meet you there.

PRAYER

God, You know the areas of doubt I have in my heart, the places where I feel stuck. I pray that You will lead me out of my doubt and into Your truth. Increase my faith and my trust in You. I willingly place my fears, my questions, and my heartache into Your hands. In Jesus' name, Amen.

FOR FURTHER STUDY

John 14:1–4
Proverbs 3:5–8
Mark 9:21–24

FOR FURTHER REFLECTION

Is there an area of your life where you're in doubt? Ask the Holy Spirit to show you where He is working in that area, and write down what you hear Him say.

Take a few moments to write a prayer of faith for that area of doubt you've been wrestling with recently.

LOVE

HOLY SPIRIT, WHAT ARE YOU SAYING TO ME?

21

The Disciple Jesus Loved

By Niles Holsinger

Peter turned around and saw behind them the disciple Jesus loved—the one who had leaned over to Jesus during supper and asked, "Lord, who will betray you?" Peter asked Jesus, "What about him, Lord?" Jesus replied, "If I want him to remain alive until I return, what is that to you? As for you, follow me." So the rumor spread among the community of believers that this disciple wouldn't die. But that isn't what Jesus said at all. He only said, "If I want him to remain alive until I return, what is that to you?" This disciple is the one who testifies to these events and has recorded them here. And we know that his account of these things is accurate. Jesus also did many other things. If they were all written down, I suppose the whole world could not contain the books that would be written.

JOHN 21:20–25 (NLT)

Most biblical scholars believe the Gospel of John was the last of the Gospels written. Most think it may have been written some 30, 40, or even 50 years after the death and resurrection of Jesus. Have you ever thought about or imagined how this Gospel came to be?

The author, a young man when he met Jesus, was with Christ from the very beginning of His earthly ministry. He was there when Jesus fed the 5,000; he witnessed the countless sick and lame brought to Him and was amazed as Jesus made them whole. This young disciple stood in front of Lazarus's grave when Jesus, ignoring the protests of Mary and Martha, commanded that the stone be removed from Lazarus's tomb. And if that isn't shocking enough, he witnessed Lazarus, dead for four days, walk out of his grave alive.

This same disciple witnessed other things too. He saw the hours that Jesus spent in prayer, and he watched as one of Jesus' closest friends betrayed him. He watched as his rabbi was beaten and pinned to a cross. He was even there, standing next to Jesus' mother as she wept, watching her son naked and dying in front of the world.

Now an old man drawing near to the end of his race, this disciple looks back over everything he's witnessed and decides to write down what he believes are the most important parts of Jesus' story.

And now, here we are. On the last day of our devotional, looking at the last paragraph of the last chapter of the Gospel of John, we come to what may have been the most significant revelation this disciple ever had.

He was the disciple Jesus loved.

John was a young fisherman who found himself part of a group of men who, at first glance, had no business being with Jesus, let alone being His closest friends. And as John is coming to the end of his life, he's come to realize that of all the amazing things Jesus did, the most amazing was that Jesus loved *him*!

We live in a time when nothing seems certain, nothing seems okay. Stress is high, patience is low, and if we were all honest with each other, we would say that there is at least one area of our lives where we aren't doing great.

But you are loved by Jesus.

Just stop for a minute right now. Take your time with this.

You are loved. By *Jesus*!

As we end our time in this devotional, I want you to think about everything you're facing right now that is causing you distress. Every burden, every problem, every broken or strained relationship. Every misstep, every sin. The truth is, despite everything you just thought about, you are accepted, and you are loved by Jesus.

You are the disciple Jesus loves.

PRAYER

Lord, You know what I'm walking through right now. I pray I would experience peace in Your presence. Overwhelm me with Your love. Show me how You see me, how You feel about me, and what You think about me. Remove the lies I have heard and unknowingly believed, and replace them with Your truth. In Jesus' name, Amen.

FOR FURTHER STUDY

Psalm 100:5
Romans 8:38–39

FOR FURTHER REFLECTION

Think about a time recently when you were not at your best. Maybe you lost your temper or said something you didn't mean. Now ask the Holy Spirit how He felt about that situation and how He feels about you.

Think about someone in your life whom you love. Maybe a spouse, a child, or a close friend. How quick are you to forgive that person? How much are you willing to give up for that person? Reflect on how that love is nothing compared to how much God loves you.

LOVE

HOLY SPIRIT, WHAT ARE YOU SAYING TO ME?

Memory Verses

"This is My commandment, that you love one another as I have loved you. Greater love has no one than this, than to lay down one's life for his friends. You are My friends if you do whatever I command you. No longer do I call you servants, for a servant does not know what his master is doing; but I have called you friends, for all things that I heard from My Father I have made known to you."

JOHN 15:12–15

3

"But the Helper, the Holy Spirit, whom the Father will send in My name, He will teach you all things, and bring to your remembrance all things that I said to you. Peace I leave with you, My peace I give to you; not as the world gives do I give to you. Let not your heart be troubled, neither let it be afraid."

JOHN 14:26–27

2

In the beginning was the Word, and the Word was with God, and the Word was God. He was in the beginning with God. All things were made through Him, and without Him nothing was made that was made. In Him was life, and the life was the light of men. And the light shines in the darkness, and the darkness did not comprehend it.

JOHN 1:1–5

1